D0492628

Understanding DNA

A Breakthrough in Medicine

TONY ALLAN

Heinemann
LIBRARY

www.heinemann.co.uk/library
Visit our website to find out more information about Heinemann Library books.

To order:

 Phone 44 (0) 1865 888066

 Send a fax to 44 (0) 1865 314091

 Visit the Heinemann Bookshop at www.heinemann.co.uk/library to browse our catalogue and order online.

First published in Great Britain by Heinemann Library, Halley Court, Jordan Hill, Oxford OX2 8EJ, a division of Reed Educational and Professional Publishing Ltd. Heinemann is a registered trademark of Reed Educational & Professional Publishing Ltd.

OXFORD MELBOURNE AUCKLAND JOHANNESBURG BLANTYRE
GABORONE IBADAN PORTSMOUTH NH (USA) CHICAGO

© Reed Educational and Professional Publishing Ltd 2002
The moral right of the proprietor has been asserted.

Produced for Heinemann Library by Discovery Books Limited
Designed by Ian Winton
Illustrations by Stefan Chabluk
Originated by Ambassador Litho Limited
Printed in Hong Kong

06 05 04 03 02
10 9 8 7 6 5 4 3 2 1

ISBN 0 431 06939 5

British Library Cataloguing in Publication Data

Allan, Tony
  Understanding DNA: a breakthrough in medicine. - (Turning points in history)
  1. DNA - Juvenile literature
  2. Discoveries in science - Juvenile literature
  I. Title
  572.8'6

Acknowledgements

BBC Hulton Picture Library, p 12; *Bettmann/Corbis*, pp 14, 15; *Corbis*, p 5 (Danny Lehman); *Hulton Archive*, p 6; *Hulton Deutsch*, p 10; *Hulton Getty*, p 8; *King's College Archives*, p 19; *Popperfoto*, p 7; *Popperfoto/Reuters* pp 26, 28; *Science Photo Library*, pp 21 (Laurent H Americain), 4, 16 (A Barrington Brown), 22 (Sue Ford), 29 (Stevie Grand), 23 (James King Holmes), 27 (Chris Knapton), 13 (J C Revy), 25 (Maximilian Stock), 17 (Science Source); *Wellcome Institute*, pp 20, 24.

Cover photographs reproduced with permission of: *Science Photo Library*, (top) A Barrington Brown; (bottom) Maximilian Stock.

Every effort has been made to contact copyright holders of any material reproduced in this book. Any omissions will be rectified in subsequent printings if notice is given to the Publisher.

Contents

Any words appearing in the text in bold, **like this**, are explained in the Glossary.

The secret of life

Cambridge, England 1953

Regular customers at the 'Eagle' public house in the university town of Cambridge were used to the two scientists who called in at lunchtime most Saturdays from the Cavendish Laboratory nearby. They talked loudly, and had many friends. One was a big, jovial Englishman in his thirties, the other a younger American. That particular day in March 1953, they seemed more than usually animated. The older man was telling anyone who cared to listen of a breakthrough they had just made, and what he was saying sounded fantastic: he was claiming they had discovered the secret of life.

The mystery of the genes

The Englishman was Francis Crick, and the American was James D Watson, and the amazing thing about their claim was that it was true. They had unlocked the mystery of **genes** by discovering the structure of **DNA**. Genes were the key to **heredity**: the passing on of characteristics from one generation to the next, like red hair, brown eyes and some personality traits. Genes could even determine the likelihood of catching certain diseases. More than that, genes separated the species: they made tapeworms breed tapeworms, chimps have little chimps, and people have human babies.

Francis Crick (left) and James D Watson relax in a Cambridge office in 1953, shortly after they had worked out the structure of DNA. Their breakthrough was a vital step on the way to understanding how genes work, and how inherited features are passed down from one generation to the next.

An important discovery

Before Crick and Watson's discovery, there had been a huge obstacle blocking all clear understanding of how heredity worked. No progress could be made until people understood what exactly DNA was and the form it took – how the chemicals it was made of fitted together. That was the mystery that the pair had finally cracked. It was a discovery that, nine years later, was to win them the **Nobel Prize** for Medicine. It was also the latest in a series of breakthroughs in the understanding of genes that another Nobel prizewinner, the French biochemist Jacques Monod, was to call 'without any doubt the most important discoveries ever made in biology'.

A group photo shows how similar looks reappear in three generations of one Central American family, from grandmother down to infant. Besides affecting physical appearance, genes also help shape people's personalities and attitudes.

THE GREATEST MOMENT

In his book *Genome*, science writer Matt Ridley sums up the world of possibilities Crick and Watson's discovery has created for people today: *'I genuinely believe we are living through the greatest intellectual moment in history. Until now our human genes were an almost complete mystery. We will be the first generation to penetrate that mystery. We stand on the brink of great new answers, but, even more, of great new questions.'*

Building blocks of life

It runs in the family

The mystery that Crick and Watson started to unravel in 1953 was one that had fascinated people for over 5000 years.

People had always known that some physical features were passed down from parents to their children, and that characteristics like red hair or blue eyes often ran in families. They knew too that **heredity** affected not just humans but also animals and plants.

From aurochs to dairy cow

From early times they had put this knowledge to use by practising **selective breeding**. This is choosing plants or animals with desirable characteristics and mating them to produce future generations in which those traits became more marked. This was the technique early humans used in the Middle East 10,000 years ago to turn the wild aurochs – a large, fearsome, big-horned creature – into the docile milk-cow we are familiar with today. Similarly, farmers used specially-selected seeds to cultivate strains of wheat that were easier to harvest than the wild varieties.

Breeds of cattle like the British shorthorn did not come about naturally. Instead they were produced over many centuries by mating bulls and cows with certain desirable features – a process called selective breeding. Shorthorn cattle like these were bred to be muscular for their beef and with short horns to make them safer for farmers to handle.

Bloodline

Over the centuries people continued to use this practical, down-to-earth knowledge to produce better crops, breeds of cows that yielded more milk and racehorses that ran faster. Yet while they had no doubt that selective breeding worked, no-one had any clear idea why. One popular notion was that the inheritance somehow passed through the blood; words like 'bloodstock' and 'bloodline' are hangovers from that error. The real nature of heredity remained an unsolved mystery.

SELECTIVE BREEDING

One of the early benefits of selective breeding may well have been in horse-riding. The first horses to be tamed, 5000 years ago, were too small to carry adults and were probably only used for carrying loads. In time, however, the largest of these small stallions were mated with the largest mares, over many generations, until eventually a breed arose that was strong enough to bear the weight of riders, revolutionizing the way people travelled.

Like physical features, some medical conditions pass down within families. Britain's Queen Victoria, shown here (centre) with some of her many relations, is thought to have carried a hereditary disorder of the blood called haemophilia. One of her sons suffered from it, and so did several of her grandsons.

Pioneer of heredity

Experiments with pea plants

The first person to work out scientifically how **heredity** functioned was not a famous scientist. He was a monk called Gregor Mendel, living in a monastery in the middle of the nineteenth century, in what is now the Czech Republic. Put to work in the monastery kitchen garden, he started **cross-breeding** pea plants, keeping careful handwritten notes of the results.

What Mendel found seemed at first to run against common sense. Most people at the time thought that if a tall plant was crossed with a short one, the result would be something in between. But Mendel quickly learned that the resulting plants – those of the second generation – were all either tall or short.

Mendel continued his experiments beyond that second crop, however, and what he found in the third generation was more surprising still. If all the second-generation plants had been tall, it seemed likely that the third-generation plants bred from them would be tall also. But they were not. They were mixed – some tall and some short – and the mixture followed a clear pattern: one short plant for every three that were tall.

The Austrian monk Gregor Mendel was the first person to discover how heredity worked. He did his research in the monastery garden, by studying how certain features were passed down from one generation of pea plants to the next.

The laws of heredity

Here was a mystery, but Mendel correctly worked out what was happening. Each young plant inherited something determining whether it would be tall or short – Mendel called this a 'factor' – from each parent, one part from the father, one from the mother. One factor was usually stronger, Mendel called it 'dominant'. But the other factor (called 'recessive') would also be passed on, and might turn up unexpectedly further down the line of heredity, maybe after one generation or even after more.

Mendel's factors are what we now call **genes**, and what he had learned about peas subsequently turned out to be true not just of plants but of animals and people too. The retiring monk in his monastery garden had taken the first big step on the path that led to Crick and Watson's discovery. He had started to unravel the problem of heredity.

This simple diagram explains how features like 'tallness' and 'shortness' can be passed on from one generation to the next.

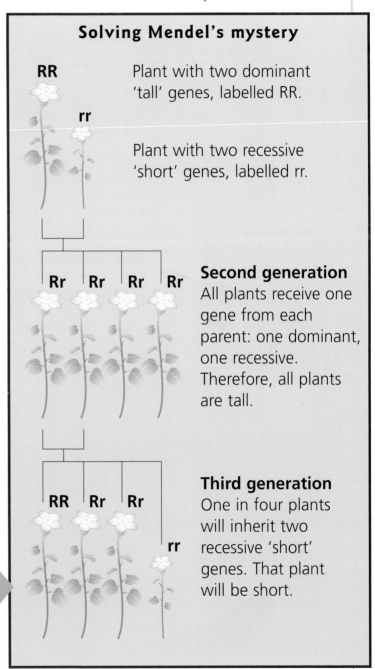

Solving Mendel's mystery

RR Plant with two dominant 'tall' genes, labelled RR.

rr Plant with two recessive 'short' genes, labelled rr.

Rr Rr Rr Rr **Second generation** All plants receive one gene from each parent: one dominant, one recessive. Therefore, all plants are tall.

RR Rr Rr rr **Third generation** One in four plants will inherit two recessive 'short' genes. That plant will be short.

Seeing small

Mendel rediscovered

Although Mendel had made a breakthrough, not many people knew about it at the time. As far as the scientific world was concerned, he was no more than an obscure gardener. He published his findings in a little-read local journal, where they failed to create a stir. Disillusioned, he turned his attention instead to his monastery, becoming its head monk. To all intents and purposes, his insights went unnoticed.

That changed in 1900, when several scientists dusted off old copies of the journal and rediscovered his work. The reason for the new interest had nothing to do with peas or other plants. It had more to do with improvements in a scientific instrument that was already 200 years old in Mendel's day – the microscope.

Looking into the microscope

As better microscopes with more powerful lenses became available, scientists were able to study smaller and smaller objects. They had known for centuries that living things were made up of millions upon millions of tiny units called **cells**. Now they were able to peer into the cells themselves – and even into their innermost parts, the **nuclei**. What they saw there called to mind Mendel's factors, which after 1900 were given a new name: **genes**. By that time the race was on to find out what exactly genes might be.

Microscopes allowed scientists to look inside cells, where the key to **heredity** ultimately lay. The instrument shown here could magnify 1200 times.

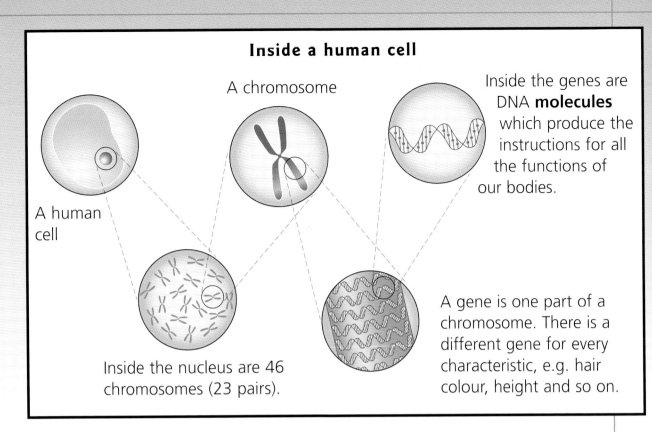

Inside a human cell

A human cell

A chromosome

Inside the genes are DNA **molecules** which produce the instructions for all the functions of our bodies.

Inside the nucleus are 46 chromosomes (23 pairs).

A gene is one part of a chromosome. There is a different gene for every characteristic, e.g. hair colour, height and so on.

Curiosity of the gene-hunters

For the most part the early gene-hunters had no idea where their researches might lead or what benefits they would bring. Instead they were driven by curiosity – the urge to solve the mystery of how life passed from one generation to the next. The answer, they knew, must lie somewhere in the mysterious dots and squiggles of the microscopic world.

For scientists could now see that the nuclei of cells contained even smaller bodies within them. There were floating, rod-like shapes that turned red when stained with dye and so were called **chromosomes**, from 'chroma', the Greek word for colour. Chromosomes themselves were made up of something even smaller. As far back as 1869 a wispy microscopic thread had been noted by a researcher investigating pus-soaked bandages from a local hospital. In time this wispy thread was recognized as **DNA**.

SECRETS OF THE CELLS

There are about 100 billion cells in the human body and in every one of them are 23 pairs of chromosomes. One half of each pair comes from the father, the other from the mother, and between them they make each of us the way we are, determining not just the way we look but also much of our personality.

A momentous meeting

Watson and Crick

James D Watson was a child prodigy. He was accepted as a student by the University of Chicago when he was only fifteen. He was just 23 years old when he arrived in the Cavendish Laboratory, Cambridge, early in 1951, where he met Francis Crick.

It was here at Cavendish Laboratory, Cambridge, that the discovery of DNA's structure was made. Work done at King's College, London, by Maurice Wilkins and Rosalind Franklin was also vital in making the breakthrough possible.

Francis Crick came from a very different background. He had studied physics at university, then worked for the British Navy, designing mines for use in World War II. He had only turned to biology in 1947, and had so far done no significant work. But no-one doubted his cleverness. Watson called him 'the brightest person I had ever worked with'.

DNA the key to heredity

Both were already interested in **heredity**, and how the instructions that shape all living things pass from one generation to the next. It was already understood by 1951 that it was **DNA** – the wispy microscopic thread seen under the microscope – that passed on characteristics from one generation to the next, and that animals and plants each seemed to have their own special DNA. However scientists didn't understand how this happened. To unravel this mystery, and discover the structure of DNA, would involve both biology and chemistry.

Yet at the time of their meeting, Crick was a relative beginner in biology; as for Watson, his background in chemistry had come to an early end as a student when he caused an explosion in a lab. As it turned out, what each of the two did know cancelled out what the other did not, and one of science's great partnerships was born.

King's College, London

In 1950 the centre of research work on DNA was at King's College, London, not in Cambridge. Another problem for Crick and Watson was that individual pieces of DNA were too small to be seen even with the most powerful microscopes. The clearest images available came from **x-ray crystallography**, and these were being produced at King's College. It soon became obvious to Crick and Watson that the path to the breakthrough they were seeking must lead through London.

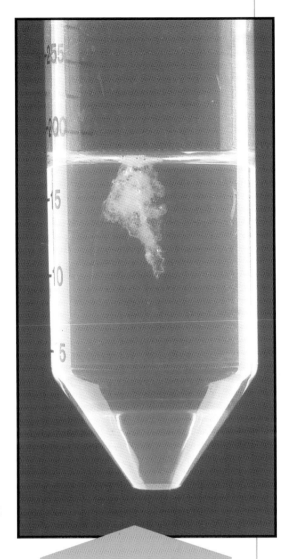

A quantity of DNA taken from white blood **cells** appears as a milky cloud in this magnified test-tube image. This sample would contain between 50,000 and 100,000 human genes.

X-RAY CRYSTALLOGRAPHY

X-ray crystallography was a technique with which people could take photographs of things too small to see even with the most powerful microscopes, including minuscule **proteins** and threads of DNA. Sadly, the results were anything but crystal clear; to most people they looked like fuzzy blurs. Yet a few far-sighted individuals realized that within them lay the secret of the **genes** – and two of those people were Francis Crick and James Watson.

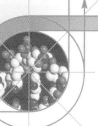

Rivals on the trail

Wilkins and Franklin

As it happened, Watson had met the head of the King's College team before he even arrived in Cambridge. He was a New Zealander called Maurice Wilkins, and it was seeing one of his images at a scientific conference that had originally got Watson excited about **DNA**.

Wilkins' principal colleague was 31-year-old Rosalind Franklin. She produced some special photographs using a technique called **x-ray crystallography**. These photographs provided the best clues to DNA's structure. When Franklin arranged a showing of her latest DNA images in London, Watson travelled down to see them. They seemed to show that the structure was a spiral, spun together from two to four chemical strands.

Born in New Zealand, Maurice Wilkins was the head of the King's College team racing Crick and Watson to crack the secrets of DNA. He had trained as a physicist, and during World War II had worked on the Manhattan Project, which produced the atomic bomb.

Watson returned to Cambridge excited. The way forward, he reckoned, was to build a three-dimensional model of DNA, blown up in scale millions of times. This would show all the facts known about the various chemicals involved and how they might link up. That seemed the best way to find a structure that worked.

Making a model

He and Crick started on a three-strand model, and were happy enough with the results to invite Wilkins and Franklin to Cambridge to ask their opinion. The visit was a disaster. Franklin in particular was not pleased to have the meaning of her own research explained to her by outsiders. She pointed out a basic error in their calculations and took the first train back to London. Word of the meeting reached the head of the Cavendish Laboratory, who officially warned Crick and Watson off further work on DNA. He feared that his government-provided grant would be cut if it was found that his researchers were working on problems already being investigated elsewhere by Wilkins and Franklin.

Competition from abroad

But Crick and Watson were not easily discouraged. They felt a sense of urgency because they knew that, besides Wilkins and Franklin, another scientist was on the DNA trail. This was Linus Pauling, one of the world's great chemists, who was working on the problem at his California laboratory. He had already put forward a suggestion for a three-strand model. Now the couple heard that he was coming to London, where he would see Rosalind Franklin's most recent photos, which could only speed him along in his research. Crick and Watson had no time to lose if they were to keep ahead of the game.

The other rival that Crick and Watson most feared was the American Linus Pauling, who was working on the DNA problem at a university in California. Watson called him 'the greatest of all chemists'.

Breakthrough!

More model-making

Crick and Watson went back to model-building. In the light of Franklin's comments, they made some basic changes to their designs. Previously they had put the chemical **bases** that were **DNA**'s working ingredients on the outside of the spiral, but now they tried fitting them inside.

Linus Pauling never came to London, but when his son Peter arrived from America to study at Cambridge, Watson learned from him that Linus was back at work on DNA. When news of Pauling's conclusions finally reached Cambridge, the two were delighted to find the great chemist had got things wrong. He still had the bases outside the spiral; worse still, he had made a simple mistake in his chemistry.

James Watson looks on as Francis Crick explains the model they produced to illustrate DNA's structure. Knowing how the parts of DNA fitted together opened the way to understanding how the messages that shape **heredity** are passed on.

Franklin's DNA photo

Then during another visit to London, Wilkins showed Watson Franklin's latest photo, of a new form of DNA. It was the clearest image yet, and it seemed to confirm that he and Crick were on the right track. On the train back to Cambridge he scribbled feverish calculations in the margin of his newspaper. By the time he went to bed that night he was convinced that DNA consisted of two strands interwoven in a spiral: a double **helix**.

THE CAT LET OUT OF THE BAG

'Then the even more important cat was let out of the bag: since the middle of the summer Rosy [Franklin] had had evidence for a new three-dimensional form of DNA. ...The instant I saw the picture my mouth fell open and my pulse began to race. The pattern was unbelievably simpler than those obtained previously. Moreover, the black cross of reflections which dominated the picture could only arise from a helical [spiral] structure.' From *The Double Helix*, James Watson, 1968

Completing the puzzle

Much work remained to be done to show the theory worked. Using metal plates produced in the laboratory's machine shops, he and Crick started assembling a model. At first nothing fitted, so the pair tried an alternative approach, joining the chemicals together in a way they had not yet tried. This time everything slotted into place perfectly. The jigsaw puzzle was complete. They had cracked DNA.

Part of a DNA **molecule** as shown by **x-ray crystallography**. It was by studying photos like this that Crick and Watson gained the insights that led to their breakthrough.

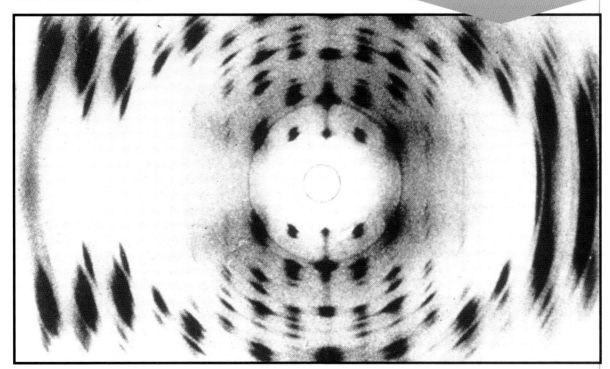

Telling the world

The staircase of life

The final model of the **DNA molecule** turned out to resemble a spiral staircase with each tread the same size and spaced at the same distance from the next. Crick and Watson had it ready to show to their colleagues by 7 March 1953, just five weeks after they had begun work on it.

Maurice Wilkins came up from London, and realized at once that the two had got it right. They half expected him to be angry with them for stealing his data, but he was generous in his support, writing to them wryly, 'I think you are a couple of old rogues. ...' So, more surprisingly, was Rosalind Franklin; once the breakthrough had been made, her hostility towards the Cambridge duo vanished, to be replaced with mutual respect as both sides came to recognize the vital part the other had played in the achievement.

Winners of the Nobel Prize for Medicine pose with their awards after the prize-giving ceremony in the Swedish capital of Stockholm in 1962. Maurice Wilkins stands far left, Francis Crick third from left, and James Watson second from the right.

TO THE SUN AND BACK

If the DNA in a single human **cell** was unravelled into a single thread, it would stretch for 2 metres. Put together, all the DNA in all the cells in one person's body would be long enough to reach to the Sun and back many times.

Franklin denied Nobel Prize

Crick and Watson revealed their findings to the world in the journal *Nature,* in an article just 900 words long. Wilkins and Franklin also each published papers in the same issue, so that their contribution should not be forgotten. It was not, and when, nine years later, Crick and Watson jointly received the **Nobel Prize** for their achievement, it was shared with a third person: Maurice Wilkins. The name that was missing was Rosalind Franklin's. It was her photos that had made the discovery possible, and it was only by a cruel trick of fate that she was cheated of her just reward; she had died four years earlier of cancer. James Watson tried to make amends when he wrote a book called *The Double Helix,* noting that in time he and Crick 'both came to appreciate greatly her personal honesty and generosity, realizing years too late the struggles that the intelligent woman faces to be accepted by a scientific world. ...' It was a generous acknowledgement of their earlier misunderstandings, and it was no less than Rosalind Franklin's due, because her research had proved to be a turning point in their work.

Rosalind Franklin died of cancer in 1958 at the age of 37, and so never got the public recognition she deserved. She had done much of the groundwork that made the discovery of DNA's structure possible.

Cracking the genetic code

Another beginning

However momentous the discovery of **DNA's** structure was at the time, it was to be several decades before it made any impact on the lives of ordinary people. For scientists, though, the discovery opened up a new world. For the first time scientists were able to explain exactly what **genes** are – stretches of DNA carrying the recipes to make **proteins,** the chemical building blocks of all life. Those proteins in turn can join together in billions of ways in different **cells**. And from cells all living things – plants as well as animals and people – are formed.

DNA, it turned out, is a code written in just four letters: A, G, C and T. These are the symbols used to identify the four chemicals – adenine, guanine, cytosine and thymine – that make it up. Inspired by Crick and Watson's insights, researchers started to

Millions of times larger than lifesize, a model of DNA's structure reveals the pattern of two linked spirals twisting around one another that Crick and Watson called 'the double helix'. In the model, the coloured spheres represent separate **atoms**.

look inside individual cells to find the chemical sequences that formed them. In the twelve years following the discovery of the double **helix**, scientists in many countries succeeded between them in working out the way in which DNA operates. Crick and Watson themselves both played an important part in this work of cracking the genetic code.

The birth of bioengineering

The next turning point came in the mid-1970s, when scientists learned how to transfer genes. They found a way of snipping pieces of DNA from one **chromosome** and then splicing them into another. Soon researchers were routinely shifting DNA from one plant to another and from animals to animals – sometimes even from animals to plants. To begin with this work was done mainly by gene researchers trying to find out how genes worked, but the technique was quickly picked up by **biotechnology** companies. By 1983, 136 of the 383 US companies using this technique were in the **pharmaceutical** industry.

This process became known as **bioengineering**, and it marked a huge step forward.

A scientist using a pipette to extract DNA from cells. Within 30 years of Crick and Watson's discovery, such techniques were becoming widespread in industry.

For it soon dawned on researchers that the new knowledge was opening up the instruction manual for life itself. Genetics would in the course of time reveal how all living things – snails as well as sea-lions, poppies and even people – are made; and through the techniques of bioengineering they could take steps to alter the process.

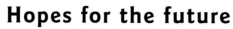

In your genes

Hopes for the future

Even though most of its benefits still lie in the future, **gene** research has opened up a whole new approach to healthcare; that was why Crick, Watson and Wilkins were awarded the **Nobel Prize** for Medicine. Its most obvious medical use lies in the treatment of **hereditary** diseases. There are over 4000 known disorders caused by genetic problems, ranging from some kinds of deafness to fatal illnesses like Tay-Sachs disease, which kills most people born with it by the age of three. At the moment the symptoms of these conditions can only be treated. The conditions cannot be cured.

Fighting hereditary diseases

Already scientists have been able to identify the defective genes that can pass on a few hereditary conditions, such as some forms of **muscular dystrophy**. This has enabled them to devise tests that can show if a person is likely to pass on the condition to their children. Before these tests were available, people who had such conditions within their family had no way of knowing this. Knowing the risks could also help individuals change their lifestyle to lessen the danger to their health.

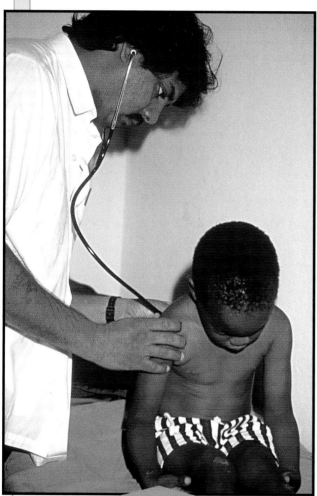

A doctor examines a Jamaican boy suffering from sickle-cell anaemia. The condition, which stops the blood from functioning properly, is one of many caused by defects in the genes. Though genetics cannot yet cure these diseases, it can help identify parents at risk of passing them on to their children.

But would people want to live their lives knowing that they have a faulty gene and could become ill at any time? Would it make it difficult for them to get jobs or insurance if employers or insurers had access to what the screening showed? Eventually these concerns may become irrelevant. Using genetic techniques doctors may be able to go beyond simply treating the symptoms of disease. They will be able to get at the root cause: the faulty message in the genes that causes the body not to work properly in the first place. They may even be able to use **genetic engineering** techniques to replace faulty genes that could lead on to other fatal illnesses, like cancer.

The Human Genome Project

A vital step in making this revolution possible has been to find and list all the genes that the human body contains. So the Human Genome Project was launched – one of the biggest scientific undertakings ever – with, at the start, James Watson heading its American arm. The aim is to map every single gene and find out where it lies in the 23 pairs of **chromosomes** found in almost every **cell** of the human body.

The project began in October 1990 and a first draft was completed in 2000. There turned out to be fewer genes than expected – about 30-35,000, rather than the 100,000 researchers had foreseen.

A scientist working on the Human Genome Project watches as a robot camera displays images of bacteria containing human **DNA** on a television screen. The project, which was officially launched in 1990, has involved hundreds of scientists in at least eighteen countries.

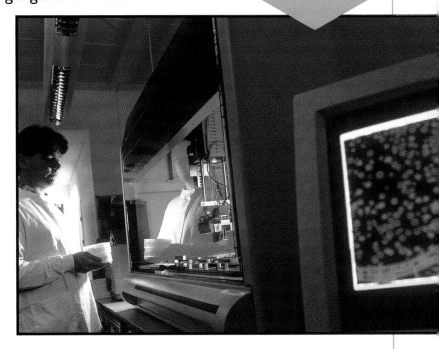

Advances in medicine

Skin grafts

While many of the possible medical benefits lie in the distant future, some advances have already been made. Engineered human skin is being commercially produced by several **biotechnology** companies. Healthy **cells** taken from a donor are used to grow new skin. Though, at present, this product is not licensed for use in all countries, it is potentially helpful for treating people with serious burns. The only other treatment is to have skin grafted from other undamaged parts of the body, which is a more painful and complicated procedure.

Making medicines

More and more drugs are now being manufactured using the new techniques. In 1982, **genetically engineered** insulin, the drug used by **diabetics**, was approved for human use. Previously insulin was derived from cows and pigs, now it can be produced to order in the laboratory.

Animals can be genetically modified to produce drugs that help treat human diseases. A Scottish team has genetically engineered sheep to produce in their milk a **protein** used to treat emphysema, a killer lung disease. In the early 1990s, a single sheep called Tracy was already making 1000th of the entire world output of the drug.

Human and pig insulin. This drug used by diabetics can now be made to order in the laboratory using genetically engineered yeasts or bacteria.

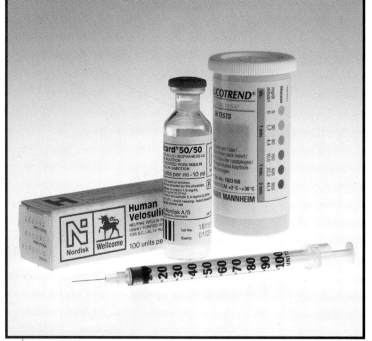

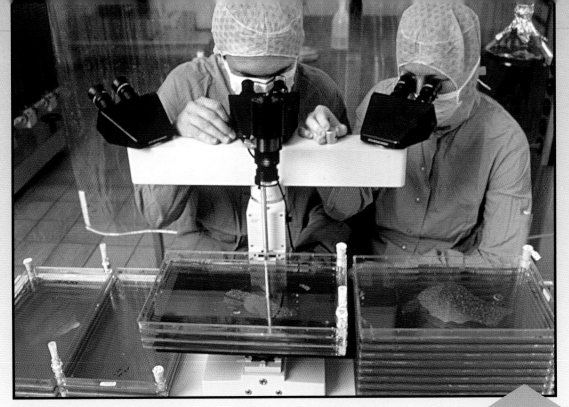

Vaccines – treatments that help prevent an illness developing by making the body build up an immunity to fight it – have been used for many years to prevent harmful diseases like polio, diphtheria and measles. They are, however, expensive and time-consuming to make. With the aid of genetic engineering they will be both cheaper and quicker to produce.

Gene therapy

This process is already offering exciting prospects for treating inherited conditions such as **cystic fibrosis**. By introducing healthy **genes** into the body cells most affected by the disease – in the case of cystic fibrosis that is the cells of the lungs – it may become possible to correct the disease.

Gene therapy could also be used to correct a person's genetic make-up even before they are born. This has been tried on mice, but not humans. Many people worry about the possible side-effects this form of treatment could have on future generations.

Laboratory researchers wearing protective clothing examine cell cultures through a microscope. The cells have had part of their original **DNA** removed and fresh DNA inserted to make them produce a protein that can be harvested for use in medicines.

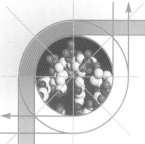

Bioengineering today

The food we eat

Medicine is only one area that the new genetics will affect. Another is the food we eat. Food can be genetically modified by removing **genes** regarded as harmful, for instance those that make vegetables go rotten. These engineered vegetables could remain on supermarket shelves for much longer, thus reducing waste and increasing profits. Scientists have already tried putting genes from a fish of the flounder family that lives in very cold waters into tomatoes, in the hope of making them more resistant to frost.

Farmers plant rice in southern China. Supporters of genetically modified foods claim that they will help produce more abundant crops – an important benefit for a nation like China with more than a billion people to feed.

Those in favour

Those in favour of genetically modified food claim that it will produce better, more reliable crops that will help feed the world's population, which is growing at a staggering 80 million every year. Already several large agricultural companies have succeeded in developing **genetically engineered** crops. They have produced potatoes which are poisonous to the Colorado beetle – an insect that can cause extensive damage to potato crops and is expensive to eradicate with pesticides. Maize has been engineered to be resistant to a herbicide, allowing farmers to spray their maize crops to kill the surrounding weeds but not the maize.

Those against

But other people are alarmed by the idea. Many fear there might be unforeseen long-term consequences to human health as a result of eating such foods. They also worry that once crops are out in the fields, they cannot easily be recalled. If the genetic agents turn out to have unwanted side-effects it might be almost impossible to get rid of them. There are also concerns about possible knock-on effects. If a bug-resistant crop is developed and all the bugs go away or starve, what then happens to the birds and other insects, like ladybirds and lacewings, that used to feed on the bugs?

Bioengineers argue back that, far from damaging the environment, the new science offers many possibilities for improving the world around us. Gene engineers are already working on biological cleaning tools that could mop up oil spills in the ocean and eat up chemical waste. There are even schemes under way to turn garbage into fuel to power factories and cars.

DNA AND CRIME DETECTION

There are many other ways, too, in which the new knowledge will change people's lives. One is crime-fighting. There are murderers behind bars today who would never have been caught but for **DNA fingerprinting** – identifying the unique DNA of human **cells** found at crime scenes and using it to track down the individuals who left it.

A researcher examines a crop of maize plants, some of which have been genetically modified so that they can be sprayed with a weedkiller. The dead weeds show up brown under the modified plants.

A fearful responsibility

Health, profits and animal rights

New hearts to replace worn-out old ones, **genes** that could help fight cancer, others that could repair faulty brain **cells**. All these ideas sound wonderful, but the way in which scientists are bringing them about can seem less pleasing. The hearts would be grown in pigs and transferred to humans by surgery. The new brain cells would come from mice. And the knowledge to fight cancer would be learned at the expense of animals **genetically engineered** to get the disease.

What are the motives behind such research? **Pharmaceutical** companies want to find cures for diseases but they are also in business to make money. This may lead to treatments being so expensive that only people in rich countries could afford them.

The world's first genetically engineered monkey, produced to promote research into human diseases, looks out on an uncertain future. Animal rights activists worry that medical advances achieved in such ways might be made at an unacceptable cost in suffering to the animals themselves.

Cloning – miracle or mayhem?

In the weird new world of biogenetics, excitement at the wonderful prospects opened up often goes hand in hand with worries about the methods used to achieve them. The doubts stretch to **cloning** – creating identical copies of animals or human beings. Scientists proved it could be done in 1996 when they produced Dolly the sheep, in effect the identical twin of her own, six-year-old mother. In theory, people could also be cloned, although in fact research on human cloning is banned in most countries. One major reason comes from the experiments on Dolly;

she was only successfully bred at the 277th attempt. There are strong objections to permitting such lengthy experiments to create human babies.

Many people, too, question why humans would want to produce identical copies of themselves. They also worry about proposals to 'improve' human children. Before too long doctors may be able to remove the genes for certain inherited diseases from babies before they are born. So far so good, but they may not stop there. It may also become possible to alter babies' genes for other reasons – to give them hair of a particular colour, for instance, or to make them cleverer. Should people be able to create 'designer babies'?

A newborn baby with its family. Scientists already possess the techniques necessary to clone human beings, though only at severe risk to the babies' health. For this and other reasons, research on human cloning is prohibited in most countries.

The possibilities that Crick and Watson opened up that day in 1953 are huge; they are also sometimes worrying. They promise to give people powers over life that they previously hardly dreamed of. Scientists in the next few years will almost literally be 'playing God'– creating new lifeforms, and altering those that already exist. The big question is whether they will be wise enough to use the powers only for the good.

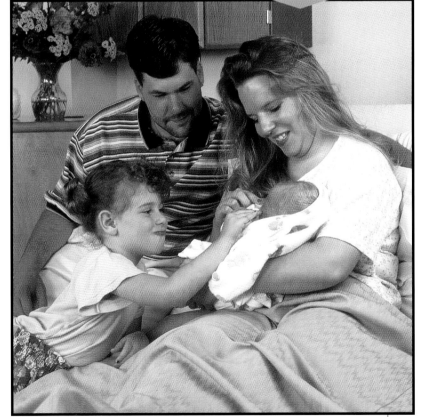

Time-line

400 BCE	Hippocrates, ancient Greece's 'father of medicine', suggests that fathers and mothers contribute equal parts of their children's heredity
1000 CE	Hindu physicians observe that certain diseases run in families
1665	Using the microscope, a recent invention, English scientist Robert Hooke observes and names cells
1865	Gregor Mendel publishes the first detailed study of the way in which hereditary traits are passed down
1869	Swiss biologist Johann Friedrich Miescher first observes DNA, calling it 'nuclein'
1882	Walther Flemming observes chromosomes and describes how they combine in reproduction
1883	August Weismann suggests that chromosomes must be the bearers of heredity
1887	Edouard van Beneden discovers that each species of plant and animal has a fixed number of chromosomes in its cells
1902	Walter Sutton coins the word 'genes' to describe the factors that carry heredity
1910	Thomas Hunt Morgan proves that genes are carried on chromosomes
1912	Lawrence Bragg develops x-ray crystallography
1944	Oswald Avery shows that DNA can transform organisms, suggesting it might be the bearer of genes
1953	Francis Crick and James D Watson work out the structure of DNA
1961–65	Genetic code is cracked
1962	Crick, Watson and Maurice Wilkins win the Nobel Prize for Medicine
1977	The first human gene is cloned
1982	Genetically-engineered insulin is approved for use in treating diabetes
1987	The first genetically-engineered micro-organisms are used in field experiments
1988	The US Patent Office grants the world's first patent on a mammal – a breed of mice biologically engineered to be likely to develop cancer
1990	The Human Genome Project is set up to locate and identify all the genes in the human body. Gene therapy is used for the first time, on a 4-year-old American girl with an inherited immune-system disorder. The UK bans research into human cloning.
1996	Dolly the sheep becomes the world's first cloned mammal
1998	A 1-millimetre-long threadworm is the first creature to have its DNA read completely
2000	The first draft of the complete human genome is published

Glossary

atom	the smallest particle of any substance
base	in genetics, one of four chemicals in DNA that carry genetic information. The bases are adenine, cytosine, guanine and thymine.
bioengineering	genetic techniques to alter living things
biotechnology	techniques used by researchers to change life forms and produce new organisms
cell	microscopic structures that make up plants and animals
chromosome	tiny packages of DNA; there are 23 pairs of chromosomes in each human cell
cloning	creating an identical genetic copy of an animal or plant
cross-breeding	bringing different strains of animal or plant together for breeding purposes; a mule is cross-bred from a horse and an ass
cystic fibrosis	an hereditary disease affecting mainly the lungs and pancreas. Until very recently sufferers usually died before reaching adulthood.
diabetics	people suffering from a disorder that, if untreated, leads to increased levels of sugar in their blood
DNA	the thread-like material from which genes are made; short for deoxyribonucleic acid
DNA fingerprinting	using DNA for identification purposes, in the same way that fingerprints have traditionally been used by the police
gene	a length of DNA carrying instructions to make proteins
genetic engineering	methods used by scientists to change the genes found in the cells of all living things
helix	a structure that is similar to a spiral
heredity	the passing on of characteristics from parents to children through the action of the genes
molecule	a tiny particle, made up of two or more atoms bonded together
muscular dystrophy	a wasting disease affecting the muscles
Nobel Prize	one of the yearly prizes awarded for outstanding achievement in physics, chemistry, medicine, literature and the promotion of peace
nucleus (plural: nuclei)	the part of a cell that controls the cell's activity and contains the genes
pharmaceutical	describes organizations that make medicines
protein	large molecules, made to genes' instructions that are the basic building-blocks of all living things
selective breeding	breeding from selected plants or animals to produce improved stock
x-ray crystallography	passing x-rays through crystals to create photographic images – a technique that can make an image of something too small to be seen by the human eye

Index

Titles in the *Turning Points in History* series include:

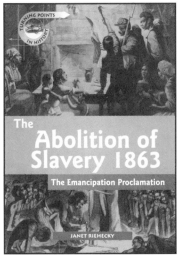

Hardback   0 431 06937 9

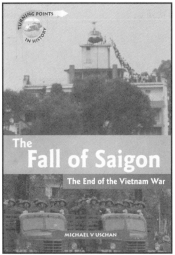

Hardback   0 431 06931 X

Hardback   0 431 06938 7

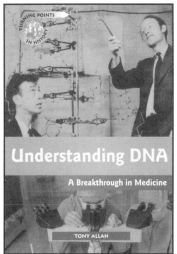

Hardback   0 431 06939 5

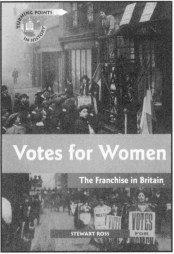

Hardback   0 431 06940 9

Find out about the other titles in this series on our website www.heinemann.co.uk/library